The Butch Mystique:
A Femme's
Perspective

by Claudia Castille

Dedicated to Angelina

Table of Contents

Chapter One: She's So Fine

I've never been overly traditional. Even when I was growing up, I was more likely to go off and do my own thing than to follow along with a crowd.

In my small town, 'preppie' high school where they managed to shove everyone from grades seven through twelve into one two-story building, this was a rarity. I'm still not exactly sure where the independent tendency came from; it was not as if my parents were either weird or uninvolved.

We had many family traditions that we followed without deviation.

Every summer we would take two vacations to the beach; one week it was to Maine, and another week to Rhode Island.

A family birthday party with cake and ice cream was required for every family member on The Important Day.

And every night, we had sit-down, family dinners at the kitchen table.
My Dad would throw out tricky words, and my brother and I loved to take turns attempting to spell them while our younger sister looked on jealously, too young (or, as Alex and I liked to tease, 'to dumb') to join in and compete with us.

My brother and I were good-naturedly united in teasing our younger sister. We figured it was the least we could do to contribute to her development, since the adults went out of their way to spoil and fuss over her.

Ours was an essentially normal, well-adjusted family, and we children were allowed to maintain our individuality and our messy bedrooms just as long as we did not encroach upon someone else.

Maybe it was that freedom which made me unafraid to do pretty much whatever pleased me as long as I wasn't hurting anyone, no matter how outrageous it was. And so I wore my entire collection of Gram's costume jewelry every day of fifth grade, green hair and faux leopard mini skirts when I got to ninth, and by the time graduation rolled around I had evolved to skintight jeans, bleached blondeness and motorcycle gloves.

Most of the other kids simply eyed up my latest style on that fresh, first day of the new school year, talked about it for a few weeks ("I can't believe she's actually wearing THAT!") and then simply chalked it up to my 'expressions of individuality'.

Anyway, if I didn't do something, it was probably because whatever it was had not yet occurred to me.

That was how it was with the butches. It took a long time for me to come to the startling realization that they were an option. For years and years, I pounded that treadmill on the man-track, searching for the perfect one that I could love forever.

Beginning with my first scruffy biker boyfriend, I could only manage to find tepid attractions for bad boys, who could at least hold my attention because they kept me guessing.

When maturity finally kicked in, some time in my early thirties, I began to develop some standards; at that point, I would only date the young, pretty boys. At least 'employed' became one of the criteria on my list, right up there below 'twenty-seven or younger'!

It wasn't until I hit forty that I felt the crazy sensation that I'd always heard people talk about but had never actually been able to relate to; butterflies.

One night, in a crowded bar, suddenly there they were, fluttering inside my stomach when I looked up from my vodka tonic and locked eyes with a tattooed musician...who happened to be a girl.

So I'm a slow learner, so what? I guess you need to practice a lot at something before you get it right.

Okay, so at the time, I didn't really know anything about 'butch and femme', much less about lesbians.

Throughout my whole childhood and up through my thirties, gayness had always been something that I knew existed but had little firsthand knowledge of, kind of like China, Lear jets and sushi.

I hadn't even known many gay people, other than my mother's hairdresser, Don...so I thought.

Until my Dad quite unexpectedly came out of the closet at sixty three. I was thirty eight at the time, and up to that point, utterly clueless.

Of course, with a surprise like that, I began to look at everyone and wonder. Before, it had never even occurred to me that women were an option. So, when I fell head over heels in love with Brandi a few years later, it was not just the emotions of love and wild attraction going on....it was a joyous explosion of my inner self, rocketing to the surface.

I wanted to sing and dance, and scream 'I've found myself at last!' to the world. It was funny, actually; I hadn't even realized before that day that I had been lost.

Brandi and I lived together for a year and a half,
during which I gradually became so jaded
with the musician thing that by the time she
moved out I was cured of any residual desire to be
with her ....or with anyone who had ever even
played a musical instrument at some point in her
life. But the attraction to butches, well...that will
never be cured.

The problem was that Brandi only looked like a
butch. She didn't have what it takes on the inside,
that elusive attitude which defines a true
butch.The 'opens doors for you, brings you flowers,
will freeze to death at an outdoor concert so that
you can be warm in her flannel shirt, and is ready
to kick ass to defend your honor' attitude that
takes the best part of the classic, two-dimensional
man and melds it with the complete, gorgeous total
package that only a woman can be.

Gina is a true butch. Brandi turned out to be...more
of me practicing so that I could eventually get it
right.

This time around, I've finally got it right. I am a
femme, so the butch/femme role thing is probably
the one tradition that I am happy to embrace.

Over the past five years, the more that I've
learned about the gay community, the more
fascinated I've become with the butch mystique.

I have interviewed ('interrogated', Gina humorously calls it) as many butches as possible, read as much as I can find about them, and just basically want to know everything! And...warning; I'm going to be very stereotypical here. Happily, unapologetically stereotypical.

Because I love everything about the Lesbian stereotypes, especially talking about them, and learning about them, and have spent many a long break at the water cooler at work, cackling with my straight friends about butches and femmes.

They love hearing about my research. They call me 'Baby L' at work, by the way, since when I first came out I described myself as a 'baby lesbian'.

Trust me, the gay world is an infinitely fascinating place for most straight folks.

One thing I should tell you is that Gina isn't my girl's real name. I've had to change it here because once everyone finds out how amazing she is, women would be pursuing her like crazy if they knew her true identity, and that would piss me off big time.

She's all mine, and I don't share.

Naturally, she loves to hear me talk like this. Another wonderful thing about butches is how much they love to be openly claimed by their femmes and Gina is definitely no exception.

There are so many categories, classifications , dynamics and rules in the Lesbian community, which pertain to both butches and femmes....although there are many more rules for butches.

Femmes are generally given pretty much a free pass on behavior, because they are femme and much admired.

From what I've seen in this area of New England, there are a lot more butches than femmes...in fact, femmes seem to be an endangered species. They are a minority and are highly sought after.

Northampton, which is a short drive up the highway, is the Lesbian capital of New England and whenever we go there I am always surprised to see so many butches and androgynous women. Not many femmes at all, and very few 'high-end femmes' like me (Gina's words when she describes me) anywhere around, and so many couples who look so much alike that they could be related!

I first became really aware of the butch-femme dynamic after Brandi moved out and I was back in

the dating arena. Not one to reinvent the wheel, I turned to the same dating process that had served me well during my man-track years, good old match.com.

Of course, this time I had an entirely different profile to put up there, and what I was looking for had completely changed. After Brandi, at least I knew that I was looking for a mate, no longer just a date.

That had been fine when I was younger, but it seemed that once I had left the world of men behind, the superficiality of those years would no longer suffice. I have come to realize that while many men (at least those I dated) are two-dimensional, women are not.

So how does one go about using words to paint a true picture of oneself, while managing to not sound so horrifyingly real that nobody in their right mind would so much as send a wink? I knew that it would be a big help to be as specific as possible about exactly what I was looking for before I even tried to wrap words around 'me in a nutshell'.

As I scrolled through the profiles that others had up, I noticed that many women shared similar characteristics. Sports was a big one! From 'enjoys playing softball' to 'Superbowl Sunday is my favorite holiday', hardly any profile seemed to lack

reference to either watching or playing some type of sport. That was a new one for me. I am decidedly non-sporty, and can't even hit a pool ball most of the time, but love of sports seems to be a common Lesbian trait.

I could definitely recognize who identified as butch, and who identified as femme, and many women went as far as to say so in their profile somewhere.

I can clearly remember that first time I clicked into match as a free Lesbian and felt the sensation of wonder at seeing how women took such delight in labeling themselves. It was like nothing I had ever experienced before.

Weren't labels something that you grow up believing are bad? To pigeonhole people, stick a tag on them, relegate them to a particular 'group' of something, wasn't that against the whole idea of individuality and being your own person?

Apparently not! A lof of Lesbians love their labels, and enjoy the perceptions that go along with them. A whole subculture has evolved and grown to be happily embraced by those who we refer to as 'Family'.

And I personally love having Gina as My Butch, just as she loves having me as Her Femme.

Chapter Two: The Femme is Always In Charge

That's what Gina told me, back before we were officially a couple, and she was giving me her take on something that another butch had said to me.

Dating etiquette as it relates to butchness is a big deal, and something that I had no idea was quite as complicated as it is. At the time, I had never felt so damn ignorant about anything before.

Thank heaven that I now have an experienced butch to teach me all the rules.

Of course, NOW she says, "geez, did I really say that?" whenever I have to remind her that what I do makes perfect sense, even when it doesn't, and anyway, it doesn't matter because the femme is always in charge, remember??

Once I began learning the rules, though, many things began to make sense. I had told her about my dating dilemmas, back when I was a single girl. About the many times had I gone out to the local club, found myself surrounded by a huge selection of obviously available butches...and been completely and totally alone the whole night.

Not one single drink had been sent my way, not a look; no notice.

I could have been dressed in a shapeless sack for all the attention I received, even on nights when I had gone out of my way to dress to impress!

This was the complete opposite from my experience in the straight world; it took far less effort to become the center of attention in a room full of straight men.

Even the most unobtrusive of men typically would muster up the courage to approach, make the attempt at conversation, offer me a drink, or ask for a dance, and with the full encouragement of the rest of the male population. 'Just Go For It!' was the common male encouragement slogan for dating.

What was wrong with the Lesbian world?

Nothing, Gina assured me. It wasn't that I hadn't been noticed.

"Believe me, " she said with assurance, "butches notice you every time you step out the door. Every time we go anywhere, I have to show the world that you're with me and you don't even notice. It's the silent butch communication that you're oblivious to because you're a femme.'

Its because the femme is in charge, and must give the sign that it's okay for a butch to approach.

"Ok, so what does that mean?" I asked in confusion. I would be out on the dance floor with my friends, casting glances here and there, noticing who was around...maybe noting the attractiveness of a butch or two in my immediate vicinity, but aside from that....well, a man would approach and make his presence known.

What was different about a butch?Why would no one meet my eye?

"Everything," Gina answered sternly. "you are the one who looks around and decides who you want to give your attention to. You make it an obvious point of catching the eye of a prospective butch; and when you do, you give a sign of invitation. Only then will the butch approach you. You have to invite them."

Wow, really? I wasn't used to that kind of respectful deference. In the straight world that I had come from, even the most unattractive man would approach a woman regardless of whether or not she had noticed him.

It was so different in the Lesbian world. I was intrigued. "Can we test that theory?" I asked hopefully.

"Not on your life!"

Damn. Oh well, guess I had to take her word for it.

But it did make sense, now that I knew more
about butches.

I only wish that I had been aware of these rules
before, when I was free to conduct experiments
to test the validity of them!

Chapter Three: Twins, or, Your Bulldog Looks Just like you!

Have you ever noticed the way that some long term couples seem to grow to resemble each other in ways that are almost uncanny?

Its kind of like when you go to a dog show and you realize that many of the dogs and their owners share physical characteristics that are surprisingly similar; like the stout little man with a bulldog tucked under his arm who looks like it could be his natural child.

That's what I'm talking about. Some couples that you meet look like twins, clones stuck in the fashion twilight zone.

Plaid shorts, matching crew cuts, glasses or not, but the identical polo shirt. They have matching runners on their feet....or it's the man-style sandals.

You can tell that they wear each others' clothing, and whats more; they even fit into each others' clothing!

Gina refers to these women as 'Plaid/Subaru Butches'.

Isn't it funny how that description simply conjures up a vision that we have all seen many times?

I do not get it. Surely they didn't look like this when they first met, fell in love and decided to spend their lives together, did they?

Try as I might, its kind of hard for me to imagine these women sneaking around, spending stolen, passion-filled hours together, locked in each others arms.

How on earth could it be possible to muster up feelings of unbridled passion for someone who looks and acts so much like great Aunt Hilda?

Where do they find the homing devices that lead them directly to THE partner who exactly mirrors them?

In the straight world, men and woman sigh over the elusive myth of finding 'the one', the perfect partner who complements them in every way...is it a myth?

Seems to be! And here, in the Lesbian capital of Northampton, they share a house and coparent a small dog, for whom they throw birthday parties and invite all their friends to come celebrate. (Yes, I have fond memories of bringing our Shihtzu to a dog party on two separate occasions; it really is a thing).

Both partners come home from their day jobs to prepare the meals and spend most evenings in

contented togetherness sharing every aspect of each other's lives, and they fall asleep in their separate beds at night.

Perfectly companionable, contentedly anticipating a lifetime of shared boredom while one goes off to her softball team and the other to her junior varsity basketball coach volunteer gig. They probably bowl with a local league together in the winter.

We've all seen these couples, and, lets face it, we've all wondered.....what is the attraction? Was there ever any attraction in the first place, or are these women so cerebral that they can completely overlook the whole 'physical attraction' piece altogether? (If so, wow, they are more advanced than I will ever be!)

And then, of course, there are the two-femme couples; women who look more like straight bff's than Lesbians when they go anywhere together.

I can't really fathom the attraction there, either. Gina thinks that's typical among closeted Lesbians who aren't comfortable being with a partner who is quite obviously gay.

After all, if only the people closest to you even know that you're a Lesbian and you're busy pretending to the world that you're straight, why would you want to out yourself by bringing a very butch girlfriend anywhere in public? It does make sense, I suppose.

Ahem, seriously, though...I would never want to be like that.

Gina and I are the complete opposite in just about everything, except in intelligence and a shared love of cooking.

We can talk about almost anything while we are whipping up some new recipe, but other than that....well, lets just say that her idea of a nice Sunday afternoon is sitting in front of a football game on television. I am not even allowed in the room during these times because I annoy her too much with my constant talking. Yes, I know; unfair! But, after all, she's entitled to her little vices just as I am entitled to mine.

She plays softball in the summer, and bowls in the winter, while I despise any and all forms of 'sport activity', including, heaven forbid, watching it.

I'd rather curl up with a good book or be debating some social issue.

She's embarrassed to be seen driving my car because of all the leopard print paraphernalia everywhere, and

insists that every cop she has ever driven by has given her a meaningful smirk.

She wouldn't be caught dead wearing makeup or carrying a purse, but she will hold mine for me, if necessary. Just for a minute or two!

Nope, we are as different as can be and I like it that way. I personally don't find much attraction at all in sameness, but I'm certainly not like everyone else.

It's a very interesting phenomenon, and it requires more research.

Chapter Four: The Uncommitted, Androgynous Type

My friend Kelly is unsure. She's not quite butch....not quite femme...and not willing to admit to either.

She completely rebuilt the deck of her house solo, swaggers like a biker in leather boots...and keeps her hair long and her earrings dangling at her shoulders.

She won't commit to being butch or femme, and when asked, will shrug and say "I'm so androgynous that neither butches nor femmes like me.....essentially, I'm screwed!"

Ok, so I say, "pick one...and go with it!" Kelly could go either way, although my money would be on the butch side. 'Soft butch' would work for her.

But on the other hand, a little bit of makeup, an upswept hairdo with a clip, and a designer purse would work the classy Sophia Loren angle perfectly.

Its all up to her, and unfortunately, she's got no idea. She hates the idea of relating to her butch side...and at the same time, finds the notion of being a femme completely alien. She rejects both.

So she remains forever on the fence.

In my opinion, the whole issue for her is one of labels. She's one of the few Lesbians that I have met who really doesn't embrace them.

She's an individual and hates the idea of putting herself in either box.

She's never been a conformist, never been one to go along with the rest of the crowd, so she rebels against what she considers 'tradition'.

In a way, its kind of like the 'fear of religion' phase that I went through back in my thirties, unfortunately its still in the process for her.

So she's almost fifty, and hasn't had a girlfriend for over twenty years.

I know, I know.....people should be free to be themselves! To be whatever they want to be, and when love finds them, they will know that they are loved for themselves.

I don't disagree with that at all—but I truly do believe that its the inner person with whom one falls in love with, the search itself is much, much harder if one hasn't figured oneself out.

And identity is a big part of that, how we express ourselves to the world.

I must admit, having always been an individual myself, it's a little bit weird to think of how fully I've embraced the traditional labels in this world.

Maybe I appreciate them more, having come from the other side. They certainly help to make some sort of ordered sense in the chaotic landscape that is romance and dating.

One thing that I have noticed is that most Lesbians definitely do date according to preference for a well-defined "type".

Certainly, the straight world has attempted to shift away from traditional labels, and I believe that its to the detriment of straight couples.

There is a lot to be said about tradition. I feel very sorry for the challenges that my friend has to contend with, and I hope that the wait will pay off and she will eventually find her princess.

Chapter Five: Straight Women

I have a surprising number of friends, all butches, who have a long colorful history of relationships with straight women which have ended badly.

Most of their stories are about a pattern of single-mindedly pursuing and winning straight women...only to have the story end when the temporary girlfriend goes back to men and leaves the butch in a bitter state of envy and jaded sourness.

Its not because all women suck, as these butches attest.

Its not because relationships are, by definition, inherently dangerous.

Its because these Lesbians have pursued women who were straight; to whom the idea of women did not occur all on their own.

These women are not drawn into the gay world by their own volition, they are lured...so, they naturally return to their own world once the novelty and excitement (i.e. 'the honeymoon') is over.

In addition, not just over but probably leaving no chance of the same woman allowing herself to step foot into the lesbian world ever again.

Many straight women in this situation eventually become so turned off by this first, negative impression of Lesbian romance that they convince themselves that the limitations of men and their predictability are more desirable then the much deeper, more profound relationships that can only be found with another woman.

Too bad for them, but understandable, really!

How many women may have come around if only they had been left to figure it out for themselves, but are instead burned and scared off by the drama of a passion paradox?

Not only are the aggressive butches in these situations dooming their own chances at ever finding a successful, long-term relationship, but they are also guilty of turning people off of the lifestyle completely, and what a shame that is!

Chris, one of my coworkers, described the long term relationship she had years ago with a woman as 'the best and worse time of my life. There was so much emotional drama that it was full of extreme highs and lows....it was completely exhausting! Never again—I'll stick with men and their lack ofcommunication, thank you very much!"

She had gone into that particular relationship directly after her cheating husband had run off with the contents of her bank account, and she was drowning her sorrow on a barstool in downtown.

An aggressive butch happened to be on the prowl in the bar that evening, and she sat down next to her.
A sympathetic ear, a couple of drinks and then...you get the picture.

They ended up in bed together, then as joint homeowners and business owners, and when it all fell apart it fell apart in a big way with the fallout spanning two cities and took almost two years to extricate from.

This was so much worse than Chris' first divorce from her previous husband.

Unfortunately, this can be a common pattern for many aggressive butches who are so hell-bent on finding a femme that converting straight women seems to be their perceived life's work.

It's really sad, because good outcomes are not very common, yet some otherwise-awesome butches can be so addicted to the thrill of the chase that they end up going in circles.

This situation is where the tendency of a lot of women to become very attached very quickly can have terrible consequences. The joke about two Lesbians meeting one night in a bar, then the next day arranging for the moving van is a real thing!

Butches be warned; but they don't usually take advice very well, which is another common butch trait.

I am a living example of why straight women need to be left to come around all on their own, as are countless other women who have come out as adults—through realization of their own feelings and needs, not by being the relentlessly-pursued object of some woman's desire.

And for those of us who end up here on our own, things generally turn out very different.

Chapter Six: First Woman Obsession

I am guilty of it, as are many of us who have discovered at some point in our adult life that we were madly in love with a woman...in the midst of our own expectations of finding forever love with some man.

All of us who have not been Lesbians for our entire lives have probably experienced first woman obsession, and the corresponding craziness that goes along with it.

For some of us, it turns us into stalkers.

Depending on our ages and experience, this could result in the kind of extreme obsession that has us setting up telephone and work surveillance, camping out at her vehicle, holding her possessions hostage.....you name it, it happens. Even to the most stable of us.

The more stories I have heard of this, the more convinced I have become that it's a sort of mental illness that affects just about every single formerly-straight woman who comes out, kind of like a rite of passage.

I've experienced it, and so have other women that I've known who came out later in life. Whats even more

relevant to the idea, though, are the many stories that I have collected from butches who have experienced this in the past with ex girlfriends.

A sort of insanity comes over us surrounding our first Lesbian lover, something that makes us act in ways completely alien to our nature, especially when it all ends.

Its as if our very first woman is an addiction of sorts, like a drug...and trying to break away from her is as difficult as it is to walk away from a substance cold turkey, even though we know how bad it is for us.

Brandi's story was the first one I had ever heard, of course, sitting in my car with my cell pressed to my ear, listening in disbelief.

Tina, her ex girlfriend, had left yet ANOTHER voice mail...number seventeen that weekend! She had even gone so far as to send Brandi a Valentine's present. It had been waiting on her desk when she walked into the office that morning.

"She sent a plant to me at MY JOB. Can you believe it? After that last time, when she attacked me outside of the club in August, I told her I wanted no contact with her ever again, and she's done this! I feel so violated!"

Tina's obsession had gone as far as parking her car on the other end of the parking lot at Brandi's office, so that when she came out at 5:30, she would see her.

She left messages on Brandi's work voice mail, her cell, and even called her mother. She would call Brandi in the middle of the night in tears, begging her to come over because she 'needed to talk'. A restraining order hadn't helped, nor had countless police reports; and whenever Brandi's band had played within miles of Tina's hometown, it could be expected that the other woman would be in the audience.

The whole situation gave Brandi a serious case of anxiety and post traumatic stress. She was always looking over her shoulder, always intimidated by the extreme emotions that Tina would display.

She couldn't seem to run fast enough, or get far enough away. And Tina resurfaced every so often for almost two years after their breakup.

At first, I was sure that Tina was a complete and total lunatic. I wondered what on earth Brandi had seen in the woman in the first place. I mean, obviously she was a nutcase, right?

The fact that Brandi had been her first hadn't even occurred to me before, or it's significance. And then, there was Brandi and I, and the way that she left me.

It was enough to make anyone become unbalanced; out of the blue, she suddenly decided she 'needed space.' So she took her clothes, and disappeared to go stay with her mother.

There was not so much as a call, a text, or even an email for the next month. I felt like my world was slowly being ripped apart, and I didn't even have a voice in the matter.

My instincts screamed to chase after her, to clutch her to me...to camp out on her mother's doorstep,the parking lot of her job, whatever it took to get her attention, to make her see me, make her sit down and talk to me, but my pride wouldn't allow it.

But, oh, I wanted to, believe me. So many times I caught myself in the act of actually dialing the phone, ready to tearfully demand an explanation or beg her to 'just come home' once she answered.

It was only iron will and angry pride that made me hang up the phone before it connected.

Jealousy consumed me; my imagination conjured up all sorts of wild visuals of Brandi off at weekend gigs with the band, frolicking in hot tubs and down in Key West with strange women. I was convinced it was happening, and as the silence stretched across the weeks, my anger and jealousy were almost impossible to control.

Silently behind the scenes, I stalked her on Instagram and Facebook, furiously monitoring every posted message that came through from some woman....convinced that every second away from me was spent in the arms (or in the sights) of another woman. I drove myself crazy!

I am fully convinced, in hindsight, that if I had been younger...less experienced by my years of marathon dating and the lessons that the man-track had taught me, I wouldn't have been able to resist the urge to chase.

I would have easily slipped into the obsessive behavior of so many others like me and become a stalker.

I managed to resist the very strong urge, but many others are unsuccessful.

These are the horror stories that we hear about so often, about the crazy ex girlfriend who can't seem to let go.

What is it about Lesbians that makes women who were once straight fixate on that one particular woman, to the point of unhealthy obsession?

There are often common threads in the relationships that carry the same story, over and over again.

Straight woman notices Lesbian and falls hard. She sets her sights on luring her. Seemingly by coincidence, the two get together. It is a passionate love affair for a short time, with both women equally focusing on each other.

Then, Lesbian begins to feel suffocated by the attention, and starts pulling away.....straight woman (like with hetero relationship with a man) gets insecure, and holds on tighter.

This only makes Lesbian run harder. Eventually, Lesbian cuts ties and disappears, leaving formerly-straight girlfriend wondering what the hell happened?And determined to find mia lover and 'fix the relationship'.

Obsessive behavior ensues; calling, gift-sending, stalking, etc. Can escalate into increasingly desperate behaviors depending upon reaction of Lesbian lover.

Old adage 'whatever you chase in life runs away' applies! Eventually, formerly-straight woman begins to get her bearings back, psycho behaviors begin to lesson.

The running slows, as Lesbian begins to miss the attention...and as the formerly-straight girlfriend draws back further and further from the relationship Lesbian misses the attention level she was getting from her girlfriend.

This need begins to slowly pull her back into the relationship.

Sometimes, it goes on for years.
Sometimes, the baby Lesbian moves on.

I moved on in a few months, and tried to put Brandi out of my mind. It took an entire year, but by the time that me and the new butch decided to call it quits, I was finally over first woman obsession.

I know very well that it didn't do my next relationship any favors, and that I was unconciously using my new lover as a bandage of sorts, to ease the pain.

We all make mistakes, and hopefully we are able to learn from them.

Chapter Seven: Femmes

Sometimes the only way to identify a femme is by the butch girlfriend standing at her side.

Even among those who have spent a lifetime perfecting their gaydar, the femme remains an elusive creature, hard to identify unless she chooses to reveal herself.

Its as if she stays camoflauged in the straight world, blending carefully....although not too much into the background.

Straight men are always hitting on her at the grocery store, and where she volunteers.

She wears dresses, high heels and makeup, and she can carry on a conversation with any straight woman about fashion and the entertainment industry.

She can provide insightful advice into relationships, dating, and what gift is appropriate for a newly engaged couple. But of course, she is much, much more than meets the eye.

Perhaps femmes are so sought after because they embody the very essence of feminity, something that butches, who are generally very much in touch with their masculine sides, desire.

They also seem to be in somewhat short supply, or
so I have been told.

Walking down the street in Northampton or
visiting a farmers market in Brattleboro, two of
my favorite haunts, I generally find myself
thinking the same thing.

Gina and I have discussed this fact at length, many
times from barstools at Diva's as we watch the
crewcuts and plaid shorts go by.

Here and there, an odd femme can be spotted, and
you can feel the attention that she generates,
even if there is no discernable notice.

At least, I can't see anything—but of course, Gina
can.

She tells me all the time that I can't cross the
dance floor on my way to the rest room without
attracting attention.

Attention, she insists, that isn't readily noticeable
because first of all, its clear that I'm with her,
and, second of all, the butch code
demands that a femme is afforded the respect
that she deserves.

The femme is always in charge, and must make it clear that attention is wanted by signaling.

"That's crazy," I scoff to Gina, "how can you possibly cast a come hither glance at someone who refuses to meet your eye because its disrespectful'?"

I can see how hard it would be to meet anyone if one party expects to be pursued while the other wouldn't dream of approaching because it might be considered disrespectful.

How in the world do women ever get together, if that's how it is? How indeed?

I have no idea, but Gina insists. There are different levels of femme, naturally...just as there are different levels of butch.

Again, it is not just what is on the outside, its an attitude as well.

Chapter Eight: Some Butch Traits

"I don't have an ego." The delivery was absolutely deadpan, spoken with such assurance that if I hadn't known better, I might have believed it.

The stunning GQ butch, lounging indolently across the tall barstool and trailing her finger across the edge of her martini glass definitely seemed to believe what she was saying.

But knowing butches as I now know them, I knew better.

I smiled and leaned forward intently. "So....what exactly does the word 'ego' mean, then?"

She released a long breath and leaned back slowly, unable to resist puffing up a little bit as she savored my interest.

One thing that all butches love is when a femme gives them attention; all have the tendency toward vanity like a Tom Turkey and will behave in a startlingly similar fashion.

"It means that I won't compete."

I lifted my eyebrow and nodded, as if I understood completely, and took a sip of my girly drink as I waited for her to elaborate.

I knew that she would, and that it was an explanation that she used quite frequently.

"Women fall all over me, all the time. I don't do anything to invite it, I just seem to always be in a situation. " she sighed.

"For instance, my assistant at work happens to be a good friend, and as straight as they come. He has no idea that his wife propositioned me one evening when I was escorting her to the bathroom at the club we were all out at. Whenever she has a little too much to drink, she drops not-so-subtle hints and invitations, and her husband is completely clueless that this is going on! But I would never, ever participate in cheating behavior." She declared forcefully.

"And its not just that particular woman; a lot of the wives and girlfriends of my friends hit on me. I just smile and walk away. No way I'm getting myself involved in those situations!"

The martini was vanishing rapidly, tossed back with the casual ease of someone well accustomed to that particular bite, as the woman went on, warming to her subject.

"Victim of circumstance! That's what I am; I mean, I don't put myself there and I don't invite attention. I walk into a club, and I know that I

could easily have all of the most gorgeous women in the room in a blink of an eye, but I'm just not going to be competing with everyone else for the attention.

I don't need it! I'd rather just sit there and be unobtrusive." GQ signaled to the bartender for a refill, shaking her head in disbelief at how wronged she felt.

The nerve of all those women, responding to all the sex appeal that she just could not help but exude. No ego at all there, clearly!

Being convinced that everyone wants to sleep with you is a glaring example of a powerful ego in action.
I have found that many butches have that quality in spades; the more macho the butch, the bigger the ego, and it usually translates into a need for attention. Especially in fields such as law enforcement and corrections, where machismo is the number one personality trait shared almost universally among those who gravitate toward these jobs.

Naturally, the dosage is different among individuals, but I've never known a cop, prison guard or court officer who hasn't had at least a little bit of macho going on.

And the more macho, the greater the ego, usually, and the greater the need for attention. Especially the sexual kind.

Ego; it's just another one of those qualities that make butches so fascinating, and attractive, although not necessarily relationship material.

Although GQ would deny ownership of this until she was blue in the face, another very defining quality of butchness that I have found is the love of competing.

Sometimes it is so pronounced that it seems like the main focus in life for some butches is competing against each other. It doesn't even matter what the winner gets, all that matters is that someone gets to win!

This is probably why so many butches love sports the way that they do.

Gina is very competitive, although she is also a graceful loser. At the end of the day, she enjoys the game, and the spirit of the competition. She loves the feeling of being a member of a team, and the comraderie. She cheers on her friends when they are playing a great game, and encourages them when they are not. Few butches would deny this quality in themselves

the same way that GQ does, and that's a good thing because competitiveness really is a wonderful defining characteristic of a true butch.

Another very common trait that true butches share is confidence.

Gina will boldly join any ball game that is being played, from basketball, to bowling, to cricket. She doesn't need to know that she is good at it, and she doesn't care whether she is or not. She is very confident in herself, and it shows.

She is willing to risk failure in order to try something. This is the essence of confidence, and butches who fully embrace their butchness have this quality in spades.

Chapter Nine: Bull Dykes

You've all seen them and been awed, impressed or at the least, slightly intimidated by the sheer, in-your-face butchness that is personified by a tattooed, muscle-bound, crewcut-sporting diesel.

I will never forget the first time I ever saw one, lips twisted in a snarl, biceps flared below snug white teeshirt sleeves and slouching casually over the tank of an old Harley lowrider.

I nearly fell off my stilettos. I turned so quickly to watch the bike and its interesting rider rumble down Pearl Street in Northampton that Gina had to steady me.

"Whhoooooaaaa....what in the world was that all about?" I hollered, hopping up and down and clutching Gina's arm so tight that she grimaced.

"That, my darling, was a bull dyke." Gina grinned, enjoying my reaction.

My brow furrowed, as I tried vainly to follow the sound of the Hog fading into the distance, "lets follow her! " I exclaimed.

The grin was slowly sliding off Gina's face as realization dawned that I had

an interview in mind. I just *had* to talk to the woman, find out a few things.

"Oh no, " she said firmly, shaking her head, as she slid her arm around me and began to gently but firmly guide me toward the restaurant where our reservation was waiting for us. "No way!"

I contained my disappointment...for the moment. But I was going to have to revisit the subject.

Most Urban dictionaries describe these extreme butches disparagingly.

'Masculine, more mannish than a man, dominant, able to kick the asses of most men...etc' but the bottom line that I think we can all agree on is that bull dykes are fascinating in a scary kind of way. They have so much attitude and are so out there, how can one help but to be intrigued?

I waited until after Gina had taken her third swig of stout. "Do you know any?" I asked innocently.

She eyed me from beneath a sharply lifted brow for a moment, then sighed.

"Of course. And yes, I will introduce you if we encounter any of them when we're out and

about." I grinned hugely. "Thank you, baby!"

Gina took a very long gulp from the bottle, then put the nearly-empty bottle down with a thump. She caught the eye of our waitress, who happened to be approaching with a loaded tray of appetizers.

"I will need another, please." It kind of sounded like a prayer, for some reason.

"You know, bull dykes only like femmes. They can be a bit raw," she said warningly. "Please promise me you won't ever approach one without me."

This time it was my eyebrow that shot upwards, "honey, you know that you can trust me!"

Gina's lips thinned, and she frowned, "it's a matter of respect between butches.

That code of conduct again.

I am still waiting for an introduction after more than a year, but I am patient. Maybe by the time I get around to "A Femme's Perspective 2.0", I will have more information on this fascinating subject!

One thing I can say for a definite, though; bulldykes are even more uncommon than femmes, at least around here.....which certainly adds to the fascination, and everyone I've asked about it agrees.

Chapter Ten: Between Butches - Some Rules

There are many interesting and peculiar butch rules of conduct. Not just with their femmes, but in general during social encounters.

Its important to note the distinction between those who are true butches, and those who are mock butches (or who only look the part, they are unable to back up the look with the proper attitude).

There is a world of difference. When I say 'a good butch', I am referring to a true butch, someone who walks the walk and talks the talk.

A butch's femme must have her every need anticipated and met instantly.

A good butch takes this responsibility very seriously, and this is one of the reasons why so many have large trucks; it is to have the room needed to carry around umbrellas, jackets, folding chairs, blankets, towels, bottled water, flashlights, trail mix, scissors, dental floss, and safety pins, among a great many other things that might be required of the particular femme in question.

One butch must never, ever step on another by attempting to assist the other's femme; that is

a clear usurpment of duties and will likely result in a challenge. I learned this rule quite by accident during an outdoor concert last summer, back when Gina and I were friends, and I was dating Donna, the woman I had met after Brandi.

As evening brought an end to blisteringly hot temperatures that had made us sweat all afternoon, the thermometer dropped a good twenty degrees.

I had not thought to bring a jacket on the odd chance that this precise thing might happen...and that didn't matter anyway, since it was my girlfriend's job to make sure that avenue was covered.

A jacket was the one thing that Donna completely forgot about. So there I sat in my folding lawn chair beneath the umbrella with my teeth chattering.

Gina, the only member of our group with the foresight to be wearing a sweatshirt, noticed me shivering and promptly handed it over.

"Then you"ll be cold," I protested in surprise. She replied firmly, "no matter. You won't be."

Oblivious to anything but how grateful I was at that gesture of extreme nobility, I happily

curled right up in it, and what a difference it made for the rest of my night! Stoic as as always, Gina finished out the remainder of the evening in short sleeves without complaint, even though it was probably sixty five degrees in that field.

I could not help but cast admiring looks her way.

Not a word from my girlfriend, but the set of her jaw told the story, and on the way home she told me that I should have refused the sweatshirt.

It wasn't Gina's job to look out for me, it was hers.

I rounded on her, "are you serious?" I demanded, "you would have preferred that I freeze rather than take her sweatshirt just because it wasn't yours? Do you have any idea how ...petty and jealous that sounds?"

Shamefacedly, Donna shook her head, "no, of course not; I was just kidding!" She answered quickly, recognizing that I was a teeny bit annoyed just then, and, since the femme IS always in charge....she certainly didn't want to make it any worse by suggesting that I should have suffered a hardship merely on a principle.

The thing was, as she referred to 'that night'
many more times whenever the subject of Gina
came up in a conversation, that she hadn't really
been kidding at all!

Months later, Gina explained how she had made
the conscious choice to overstep her bounds by
giving me her jacket.

She was breaking a butch rule. She confessed
that she knew she was risking a confrontation,
but had gone ahead and done it anyway.

"I couldn't let you sit there shivering and
uncomfortable just because she failed to
provide for you!" Gina declared hotly, "I was
looking at it in terms of the cardinal rule, the
rule that trumps all others, which is that
femmes must be taken care of."

The mark of a true butch, one cardinal quality, is
that she is a gentleman.

Well, in retrospect, I guess I can understand
why my girlfriend had been so annoyed, even
though I had thought it completely charming
and gentlemanly of Gina.

"you must have been freezing," I told her.
She laughed, "course I was! But I hid it well,
didn't I? I had to show my butch toughness."

How could I not be impressed? She had broken a rule for me, putting my comfort above butch protocol...I couldn't help but feel even more cherished. She's a keeper!

And to think, that was before we were even together.

Learning about the rules has been fascinating. I remember another event that happened last summer.
Donna and I had gone to a barbeque and pig roast at a huge outdoor venue somewhere down in Connecticut with some friends.

Beer, cobbed corn and hamburgers were plentiful, and people were dancing to the very zippy country band that was playing. Everyone seemed to be in high spirits, having a great time, and it was like old home day for members of our group as people kept coming up to us to say hello.

There was one rugged butch who stands out in my mind strongly because when she was introduced to Donna and me, she looked right at me and said hello, but when she was shaking Donna's hand, her eyes were trained somewhere over her shoulder.

It was very obvious, and I noticed. As she walked away, I whispered to Donna, "you know each other, don't you?" Donna shook her head, and I hissed, "Then why didn't she look at you?"

"When two butches meet, their eyes don't connect, they just shake hands." she answered.

This is one lesson that younger butches who are just learning the ropes quickly learn, when they find themselves being put firmly into their places by a seasoned veteran.

There is a definite pecking order, and a deference to age and butchness.

Two butches will never arrive at a door at precisely the same time because this would require a challenge where the 'winner' earns the right to put her hand on the knob.

Instead, one will fall back and immediately turn her attention to her cell phone, acknowledge an acquaintance, or any kind of other diversion that delays her slightly.

Butches are very careful not to step on each others' toes.
The whole challenge thing is fascinating.

 Chapter Eleven: Accessories and Other Symbols

Most straight woman completely understand the concept of accessorizing, and I, like all femmes, share this arcane knowledge.

Fashionable pumps, matching purses, hairstyles, makeup, nice clothes; in my former life as a straight woman, I became very experienced in all of these items.

One of my favorite styles is leopard print, and trust me, my car is all decked out to the nines (Gina will ride in it, but she hates driving it). In other words, I'm pretty girly!

It's a fairly straightforward language, and femmes all speak it to some degree, although some are more fluent than others; all the tools are the same as used by straight women across the world.

For butches, it's a little bit more nebulous. What is the best way to use symbols to display one's butchness?

Straight men, for the most part and especially out here in the country, tend not to be quite as concerned with accessories.

The obvious exception is of course, the metrosexual male, but there aren't all that many of those around here.
Generally speaking, when a male in this neck of the woods turns up obviously coordinated, the first assumption that
everyone makes right off the bat is that he must be gay. And usually, its true.

Among straight guys, less is more, the old saying goes...and that definitely holds true in New England!

However, in the more metropolitan areas, the same man would not be viewed in any way differently than any other. It really all depends on the area, I suppose.

Butches tend to dress and accessorize the same way that men do; they are more in touch with their masculine sides, after all.

Cologne and tattoos are probably the most universal symbol these days, and you hardly find a man or a butch who doesn't make good use of both. For many of them, that's it. But of course, that's just the tip of the iceburg

Butches shop in the mens' sections, and have subscriptions to 'The World of Wood' and 'Sports Illustrated'.

They carry a wallet, not a purse. And no self respecting butch would ever wear makeup.

Before Gina and I were together, during the many months that we maintained a long-distance friendship, she asked me for my femme advice about what to wear going out. My first response was, "motorcycle boots, a thick leather belt with a big buckle, and a white coral choker necklace."

I'm a sucker for leather boots, especially because they make my butch even taller than normal and I enjoy that feeling of being dwarfed by her physical presence.

The belt part is because long before we were together, I entertained myself with fantasies of her reaching up to unhook it for me, and hearing the audible 'click' when it released. I'm very auditory.

Believe me, I had a whole library of erotic scenarios involving me and her, for months and months during the last six months that I stoically remained with Donna.

Those fantasies were what kept me going...but I digress!

Back to accessories....Anyway,the choker was a particular accessory that I thought would look

very sexy around her neck; she has a solid, strong neck that is just one more thing about her that I find soooo attractive.

I've always liked the look of chokers on muscular, suntanned necks....both male and female, depending on the era, call it a fetish! And I knew that Gina would definitely wear it well.

Sure enough, the motorcycle boots were totally her style, and so was the light leather jacket she threw over her tight, crisply-white man's t-shirt.

I was right on in my assessment of what would be a good style for her....the James Dean look was definitely her.

I could not resist gifting her with the white coral choker that I had acquired in Jamaica the previous year; it was really so her. The choker added a little laid-back element to the look, and was another definite 'yes'.

Once we were officially together, I could be a little bit more aggressive in accessorizing my girl.

We went shopping for a new, manly-smelling cologne for her, and as the months passed, her hair got shorter and shorter, acquiring a rakish spike on the top which so suits her.

"Jenna told me that I look like a chicken!" she announced proudly, bursting through the front door carrying a large bouquet of sunflowers, my favorite. Jenna is her bff.

I frowned consideringly. The spike did stand up with great energy, perhaps a teeny bit similar to a cock's crown, but just a teeny bit. To say it was like a chicken was really a stretch, in my opinion.

Gina, however, wasn't at all bothered by the opinions of others. She really only cared what I thought, which is fitting!

As she filled me in on the various reactions she had gotten from the members of her softball team when they saw her new hairstyle that afternoon, she was more animated than I had ever seen her.

"And I actually got carded when we went to the restaurant after practice; first time in over ten

years that's happened! Can you believe it?" she crowed, "no one my age has a hairstyle like this, its unheard of!"

Accessories go a long way in contributing to the butch mystique. They should never be underestimated, and any good femme has a responsibility to ensure that her butch is sporting the best look for her.

Take control of the situation whenever necessary. Remember, the femme is always in charge!

 Chapter Twelve: We Are Family

Have you ever noticed that in Lesbian communities, it seems that many members of friend groups have either been in a relationship together or slept with each other at some point? And not only that, but you could fill a football field with ex girlfriends who remain close friends.

This is something that is much less common in the straight world. Men and women walk away from each other and often have no further contact unless they have children together.

Lesbians break up and the ex winds up renting a room in your house for the next five years. Even more strange; the new girlfriend is actually okay with that. Both new girlfriends are okay with it; yours *and* hers.

Is it just me, or is something odd about this picture? The Lesbian community tends to be what I call incestuous. They call it being close-knit.

This is not only because there are fewer fish in the local pond, but also because we have a tendency to do everything together within our little social groups.

These are the people that you know, so these are the people who you end up having relationships with, and since there are so few of you, you maintain contact after. Also, women place a high priority on relationships anyway, so women don't like to let people go.

In the straight world, the girl honor code doesn't allow you to go out with your best friend's ex boyfriend, unless:
a.) you have discussed the situation at great lengths with her and b.) she has no problem with it.

If either of these two conditions is not met, it simply can't happen, and usually doesn't.

This rule does not apply to the Lesbian world, and it does happen more often than you'd think!

They've definitely dated some of your friends, and many of your friends dated amongst themselves at various times as well.

Most of the time, normal Lesbians remain friends with all their exes. You could (and very often do!) fill a dancehall with all the people that are tied together as a result of being an 'ex-this' and 'ex-that' of Lesbians.

Sometimes, the new partners resent it and it causes drama; most of the time, though it is simply an accepted fact that your new girlfriend is probably close friends with her ex, and her ex's family, bff, and so on.

This has been one struggle that I still find hard to wrap
brain around, but I'm working on it. It is probably a result of my residual straight world conditioning.

At the end of the day, its a prioritization of community, and that does feel like a good thing.

It also speaks to a real need to always work on your own mental health, especially when you're dealing with a breakup, so that you are in a good space and can appreciate the community support aspect while not getting pulled down into jealousy and other painful emotional reactions.

This is one of the powers of the feminine principle.

Lesbians seem to have gotten it right.

Chapter Thirteen: P'Town - IS it A Mecca?

Ok, so many Lesbians are going to get pissed off at me for this chapter, but its not in my nature to hide or pretend that I feel differently than how I feel. This chapter isn't about butches, either, but its relevant.

I have to tell it like it is, even if it goes against popular opinion. I'm always getting into trouble with someone, and you know what? That's just life! And I do have my reasons.

I've long heard stories of how wonderful Provincetown is, how it resembles a piece of heaven on Earth to the gay population in the American northeast.

Practically every Lesbian I've ever encountered has been there and has something to relate, some particular experience that happened there at some point in her life.

It seems to be THE place to get away to; the place where everyone wishes she could actually live year round.
There's even a publishing company with an entire library of Lesbian-romance novels that was born out of a single vacation in P'Town and has grown into one of the biggest publishers of our genre.

There is definitely something to be said about the energy of being in a town where you are amongst people who all share the same core lifestyles.

My first visit to P'Town was with Donna on last year's Memorial Day weekend, which hallmarks the kickoff of 'the season'.

Gay people from all over the place flock to P'Town to welcome Spring, say goodbye to winter, and to walk up and down Commercial street, day after day.

There are numerous shows going on in the various establishments; famous gay comediennes, adult-only drag shows....basically if its entertainment and its gay, then its performing somewhere in P'Town and very likely during the Memorial Day weekend. Brandi's band plays there now and then.

You can find any sort of fetish, any butch accessory, and any romance novel available in one of the numerous little stores on the main road or down a little side street, and of course all the regular items are for sale, too. Artwork, housewares, clothing, meditation aids, gourmet pet treats....all these things can be found without much effort within a short distance.

You can participate in Drag Queen Karaoke over at the Governor Bradford's Hotel bar with a very foxy queen in six inch heels, and really let down your hair to the latest hip-hop music over at the Vixen.

The smell of fresh breads and pastries baking mixes with the salty air in the early morning, and as the day rolls on in, it takes on lobster's savoriness.

No matter what it is that you want, you can find it in P'Town.

"Wow," you say, "all of that and gay people, too?"

Uh huh, especially gay people. Everywhere that you look, couples are walking together holding hands; gay men and Lesbians.

In the clubs and bars, the singles scenes are hot and full bore; just like the downtown clubs in most major cities around the country, only here its mostly all same-sex couples.

Being gay isn't just accepted, it's the fashion. Straight people come here just to be amazed, and virtue-signal their open-mindedness.

For many gay people, it's the only place that they say they feel they can truly just be themselves, without any reservations or censure. In P'Town, they don't mind if anyone looks at them holding hands with their lovers.

They are the majority, not the minority here. And that's very different than the typical experience that happens out in the rest of the world. Many of them cannot wait to get back to P'Town every year; they live for it.

I get it, I really do. It must feel awful to have to live closeted lives, unable to openly talk and share personal stories with co-workers. Many of the older generation still introduce their life partners to their relatives at the holiday get togethers as 'my friend'.

I understand that these things do still go on, and are very real.

Many gay people truly fear that when the important people in their lives, friends and family, actually are confronted with the undeniable fact of their gayness, that they will be shunned and rejected, and this is also a sad truth in many cases.

I understand that these are things people feel and these are their realities. I also understand why they feel that in order to be able to truly relax, they are willing to do whatever they have to do in order to spend time in a place like P'Town, which caters to that need and insecurity by overcharging and taking financial advantage whenever possible.

The same lobster dinner in P'Town costs half of what they sell it for at a fish fry in my little Western Mass hometown.

It even costs more than lobster in a Maine, and Maine is the place that everyone goes to for lobster!

I can get a pint of beautiful sea scallops, batter fried to perfection, for fifty per cent less than what I would pay if I were sitting on the deck of a restaurant at the junction of Commercial street.

The same sweatshirt with "P'Town Crewe' splashed across the chest costs thirty dollars in the 'Denims' store on Main Street that would cost $70 in a shop in P'Town.

Opportunists always seem to know the vulnerabilities of people, and they find the best

way to exploit them. With the gay population who are drawn to Provincetown, they have the perfect gig and they take full advantage of it.

This is what bothers me about P'town, and why I am not impressed by it. I actually think that its even more overpriced than other typically touristy spots because of the innate desperation that drives the gay population; this is a unique phenomenon that is not shared by the straight population.

Its an accepted exploitation of gay people.

I certainly don't hold it against anyone who feels the need to get away and be surrounded by like-minded people. I can totally relate to that. I understand.

However, to me...walking down the street holding my girl's hand is second nature and I don't even think about what people think. We sit side by side at the local watering hole frequented by my coworkers from the office, and at any time there's the danger that when our eyes meet and hold for too long, someone's tongue will end up in the other's mouth. This is just a regular occurrence. It does not even cross my mind who might be watching, or what that person's

reaction might be. I simply do not care, as long I'm surrounded by adults, of course.

I don't need to be on Commercial Street to walk with my arm around my girl's waist and my hand in her back pocket; this is how we walk whenever we are out and about and no matter where we go.

I also understand that the way that I am is far from representative of the 'typical' over 40 Lesbian.

And I also live a half hour from Northampton, the Lesbian capital of New England. A huge percentage of the residents there live with their same-sex partner, so the population contains a large segment of the population that is gay.

Walking down a street in NoHo with straight friends, I know that the assumption of everyone that we meet is that we are all gay, and I find that highly amusing. But as long as I've been coming here, its been the rule...not the exception like it is everywhere else.
, again, where I tend to hang out is a place where everywhere that you look, you tend to see as many if not more same-sex than hetero couples, and so I don't feel out of place anyway.

I don't like it when people take advantage of others, or when they exploit the vulnerabilities of others in order to make money.

And P'Town, to me, seems like a place that is generally involved in doing just that, especially when it comes to making as much money as possible in the process.

A lot of members in our community struggle, and live hand-to-mouth. They should not have to tolerate being exploited just to take a vacation and to feel accepted and safe.

It's a sad world that we live in where this is the norm. And that's my take on P'Town. Sorry. I wish it was different, but it's what I see.

Chapter Fourteen: Hang Ups

This chapter is about a sensitive topic that I have learned is quite common to butches, and so it has relevance to the Lesbian community overall. I've talked to many people, and have gotten many similar stories.

First off, let me say that for two people with no issues or inhibitions whatsoever to get together, fall in love, and actually have a meaningful relationship where there are absolutely zero hang-ups to overcome practically requires an act of God. Its that unusual, and especially now in this age of rampant mental health challenges.

There, I said it. Even during my days on the man-track, I observed that particular phenomenon and was dismayed by it.

Isn't anyone well-adjusted these days? I've noticed that a lot of Lesbians have hang-ups about themselves, which naturally carry over into hang-ups about sex, touching, being touched, intimacy, and so on.

Many have had profound abuse in their pasts. Many have had to deal with growing up repressed, and/or growing up in a secretive or hostile family

situation. At the very least, most have had some experience where they felt shame, and a total lack of acceptance. If these issues are not resolved and healed, they continue to have great impact on emotional well-being.

Hiding behind a mask is being in denial of your authentic self. It saps your energy and depletes you.

Its like holding a pose for an extended period of time. You can't relax. Even if you've trained yourself to present a certain way and you think its completely instinctive, a small part of you must still devote attention to maintaining that pose.

That's energy and focus that has to be directed somewhere other than on the here and now, and the living in the moment state of being that true happiness requires. Think about it!

Anyway, back to my topic. As we know, I came flying out of the closet in joyous celebration, and embarked upon a journey of exploration.

Of course, it started with Brandi, and at the time I had no idea that she and I wouldn't be together forever after, or that she wasn't the have-all, end-all when it came to sex. I had a lot to learn.

From the very first time, she was all about giving me the best experience possible, every time. She

wanted to give. She never wanted to receive.

It wasn't very long before I realized that she couldn't receive. She didn't want to be touched. Not even by me.

Brandi had a very abusive childhood, and she had never healed from it. It carried over into the bedroom. The only touch that she was comfortable with was the touch of her own vibrator.

Donna, on the other hand, was fine with being touched....but she had never had an orgasm in her life, and even with all my skill, I couldn't get her there. Same thing with Isabelle, who I dated very briefly in between Donna and Gina.

In the many authentic conversations that I've had with friends in our community, this theme is described over and over again as Women have talked about past relationships and their experiences.

Moe couldn't. Alys couldn't. Jess hadn't. Trina couldn't even stand to think about it. And on...and on....and on. All these women are butches.

It's very common. And that is a tragedy. I was surprised and very happy to find that Gina had no issues whatsoever. I don't have any issues either. We are lucky. We're also in the minority, it seems.

Granted, my research into Lesbians, and specifically butches has been very informal, and I began doing it because I was interested and intrigued by the butch mystique.

In doing so, I uncovered things that both dismayed and surprised me.

During the year and a half that I spent with Brandi, I was forced to get used to one-sided sex.....and even that eventually faded away.

It had lost most of its appeal anyhow.

Sex has to be a mutual expression of love and trust to be satisfying and sustainable. So many Lesbians eventually fall into the trap known as "Lesbian Bed Death", and it's a very sad place that I don't ever want to be in. No one should!

Why do Lesbians settle for this?

This is one area where I am left with more questions than answers, and I hope that more people will start to become aware of it in the future, and help others to find healing in ways that bring lasting changes.

This is one area that I believe men do a better job prioritizing, and we can learn something from them.

Chapter Fifteen: Wedding Bells

Hooray for all the states and especially the New England states who have legalized gay marriage; may the rest of the country soon follow suit. This has certainly cemented my opinion that the northeast is the most open-minded and accepting place to live, and I'm staying!

Of course, since my entire family lives here and has for generations, it would be hard to leave if I wanted to, but I'm glad that I don't want to, just saying.

Anyway, for years now, I've been studying the whole Lesbians and marriage theme and its very interesting to find how people view marriage.

I've always existed in a world where marriage was a possibility. Growing up in the straight world, naturally it was kind of the 'pot of gold at the end of the rainbow' dream that I shared with millions of other women on the planet.

That rainbow, of course, wasn't a Pride Flag to me at the time. When I fell in love with Brandi, gay marriage had been legal in Massachusetts for quite a few years already, so the dream remained intact as I stepped out of one world and into another.

I have not had to face the cold hard fact that I would never have the ability to achieve that dream, like so many who had grown up in the gay world.

Yet, for those who have always known they were gay, it's a completely different story, and the prevailing attitudes about marriage seem to be mostly fall into two polar opposite courts.

Some people look upon it as the ultimate expression of commitment, something even more precious because of what had to be endured to make it an option available to gay people. A battle won, a victory to be esteemed and held in high value. Sacred.

Other people look upon it as popular and what everyone else is doing, so they want to experience it. Kind of like the desire to acquire a new iphone, or the latest piece of technology. I want to have it, simply because I can, is the new mantra, and there is little thought behind the meaning of it.

This is more commonly found amongst the younger generations, who have grown up with technology and instant gratification.

Course, instant gratification is the flip side of 'disposable', and new is just as quickly and easily discarded once it is no longer new.

And, I'm sorry to say, I'm finding that it isn't even the younger generation who make up the largest percentage of people that feel this way, its still my generation. Add in the tendency to leap without looking, and it's no wonder there's a "drive through" wedding chapel in my home town.

Because it was never a remote possibility up until a little bit more than just a decade ago, and now it's fast and easy, its becoming just another thing, and hardly holds any weight. Lesbians are getting married and divorced with as much thought for the long haul as they apply when they hook up and are moving in after only knowing each other for a few weeks.

These two attitudes are the opposite ends of the spectrum of the views on gay marriage.

Of course, there are varying degrees of separation in between, some Lesbians view it casually as an 'easy come, easy go' type of thing....after all, it wasn't something that they grew up looking forward to, so therefore it was never viewed with the seriousness that it always has been in the straight world.

Sadly enough, that attitude does make perfect sense. If you're not taught to hold something in regard, the feeling isn't going to be magically produced.

A danger of marriage for Lesbians, so much more pronounced for us than it could ever be in the straight world is that women, being far more emotional, are less marriage-shy than men in general.

We are more apt to take the plunge on the spur of the moment and with less real soul searching as to whether its what we truly want for the long term. Thus, many Lesbians who were quick to run to the altar once
became legal in many of our New England states have been just as quick to join the ranks of the newly divorced when the relationships went sour.

For men, marriage has always held particular significance; and in general, men do not take the thought of marriage lightly. This very basic difference in the sexes has led to a markedly different pattern in how these relationships play out in the states where marriage is now an option.

Only time will tell how it all evolves.

Chapter Sixteen: Conclusion

Here ends what I've learned so far in this quest for information. I hope that you have enjoyed reading it as much as I've enjoyed writing it.

I started this project about seven years ago, and put it aside to focus on a Master's Degree program.

In the interim, Gina and I got married....and divorced.

Then Covid happened, and the world changed.

I don't know what prompted me to go back and revisit it now, in 2023 but as I was going through my draft, I was taken back to those early years when Gina and I were young and beautiful, and we loved socializing with our community.

I could feel again the excitement and the wonder that I felt back then.

I felt very grateful to remember. To remember Gina, and how things once were between us. And I knew that I would publish this, even as short as it is, because it really expresses the magic of what I truly believe was the most light-hearted, passionate, fun and intense time period in the Lesbian collective. We harmed no one; we only

wanted to be free to express ourselves authentically, and love who we loved freely.

Many beautiful things have been lost forever, but the experiences that we had, the emotions that we felt....they will remain for always.

I loved our community. I loved our friends. I loved our life. No matter how many changes happen in the future, I will always be thankful for the gift of that time.

And there will be many beautiful new things in the future.

I have changed so much. Our community has changed as well. Many of the things that we used to take for granted are gone.

The veils have been lifted from many of our cherished belief systems as the dark undercurrents of politics continue to churn, bringing revelations to the surface.

Those who we once staunchly believed had our backs have been shown to be wearing masks to hide self-serving agendas.

Friends have turned against friends, pitted against each other by ideological differences. Many fractured things will never be whole again.

But dawn will come again, as it always does. And the Community, battered and bruised, will come back together.

That's the power of Sisterhood.

Claudia Castille (not her real name either) lives
in Western Massachusetts. She has one
daughter and an assortment of animals, both
indoor and outdoor.
Although she is no longer a part of the
Community, she misses it every day.
But you can never go back.
You can only go forward.

Go forward boldly.